Life Unfolded

Vinita Jawahar

BookLeaf Publishing

India | USA | UK

Made with ❤ on the BookLeaf Publishing Platform
www.bookleafpub.in
www.bookleafpub.com

Dedication

I dedicate this book to my daughter Priyanka and son Siddharth who had faith in me and encouraged me always .

Preface

I thank my Husband Sanjeev for being by my side always.

Special mention of Punam who encouraged me to write my poetry and take it to next level . And all the forums that gave me a platform to pen my thoughts more openly.

Acknowledgements

I acknowledge all the people I met in my journey of life who made me write in words and prose . I Thank All Of Them .

What Poetry Means to Me ...

Poetry Brings Cheer !
When darkness falls and days seem bleak,
In poetry, solace I seek.
With words that dance and dreams that soar,
I find the light I am searching for.

Through verses woven with hope's thread,
I paint a world where hearts are fed
With joy and laughter, love and grace,
A sanctuary in words I embrace !

So let my pen become the light,
Illuminate the shadows, fight
the gloom with lines that brightly shine,..
In poetry, true joy I find !

I Dared To Dream

Should I dare to dream ..
Putting my thoughts that flow like a stream !
Yes I dare to dream -
To live my life as I feel
To shape My World
To chase the Gleam !

My words take flight
My moods and emotions in sight
Good , Bad or Right
Should I dare to Dream !

Unfolding all I want to be
In every step of dance
I want to be free ..

Through every tale
Through every rhyme
I weave through the
Sands of Time .

I Touch my Soul
I bare my heart
I Script my path ,
For My life is mine n mine to feel.

No chains to bind ; No fixed script to live
No Fears to tame !

Love to ignite my flame .
A Dream I live
A Dream that's Real

Yes ,I DARE TO DREAM!!!!!

My Life

As Time lapses into Seasons
I wonder ....
Why am I living without a Reason !
When the Nights are lonely and depressed ,
Days are long n dreary
Alone am I from Within !

Loneliness gives so much fear
So easily it brings Tears ...
So helpless I feel in my life,
Losing all my zeal to Thrive !

I long to hear a Sound
Just to have someone Around!
Laughter n shouts
Happiness n giggles in bout .
I Long for all this. ...

Such is the plight of so many people I found ..,
Let's Reach out

N Touch someone in Need
For behind a strained Smile
Someone is falling Apart by A Mile .!!

Nature's Song of the Night

The silent night,
gazing at the sky,
The black velvet sky, with millions of stars, embraced
me.

The rustle of leaves in the night breeze,
The occasional sound of crickets-
A whispered melody, a lullaby of the wild.

I lay...
Till I spotted the glow of ember—
The rising sun, painting the horizon gold.

In silence, I drifted into light slumber,
Only to be woken by the chorus of dawn—
Chirping birds, the breath of morning air,
untouched, pure, and free.

Optimism

When the going is not right
Life around might seem too tight
Feelings and Things seem dim in sight !!!

Look up at the Sky
Focus your vision to see
The Silver Lining around the Cloud
Make that affirmation Sound
And say Aloud
I am Happy n Bright !

Never to Quit
Especially when low
n hardest hit !
For
God helps those
Who help themselves!

Even as you sigh
Never leave your SMILE !

Journey

All the roads I have travelled...
The journey to oneself is the best.
The journey seeking the truth within !

The road is not always smooth
It has its bumps
In throat many a lump
In Sadness and in happiness too
But I have learnt to seek the Blessings
In my journey back to Myself !

I walk, I fall, I rise,
Through each lesson, love, and test,
Of all roads I have wandered,
The journey to myself is the Best!!!

Wish

I want to go out and enjoy ,
Dance in the moonlit night,
Beneath the stars so bold and bright.
To bask beneath the Winter sun,
And greet the Spring when blossoms come.

Though running may not be my way,
I'll walk on grass, feel light and play.
Let laughter ring, let joy remain,
Through Autumn's gold and Summer's rain.

Miles may shorten, steps grow slow,
But strong I'll stand, with heart aglow.
Friends and family around
With Happy n cheerful sounds !!
That's what I want - when ever I turn Old ...

And when the time for rest is near,
Let not there be sorrow
nor shed a tear.

Just let me go,
Before my light forgets to glow.
God , please embrace me into your fold !!

Life is a Story

Life is a story—write it well,
In ink or pencil, time will tell.
Edit chapters as you grow,
Embrace the highs, learn from the low.

Erase the lines that fade
Lines that bring you pain,
Let go of guilt, release the strain.
Rub off the doubts that cloud your mind,
Seek the truths you're meant to find.

Compose each page with love and grace,
Let courage fill the empty space.
For in this tale, you're the author true,
The pen is yours; the choice too !

So craft your narrative, bold and bright,
Illuminate the darkest night.
Humbly take It too. !
Life is a story—make it yours,

Fill the pages with love and light,
For every chapter isn't written yet
More is yet to come ...

Life is Sublime

Life is Sublime
The vastness of Eternity
The expanse of life
Can it be measured in years ?

Why do we live in such a fear ?
Death is Inevitable !

Not with a heavy heart ,
But reverence
And bountiful of beautiful memories
Lets bow and bid Goodbye ...

Make life a melody
In the semblance of a happy tune
So that it's never lost
Even when one is Gone !

Life is like a Book

Life is like a book
Keep turning the pages to have a look !
For each new dawn brings light to stay !
In joy and sorrow; hope and fear ,
Our life's tale continues ,
ever so clear !

Embrace each chapter
Some short , some so long .
Making ones Life a great book .

And truly, here we belong ;
From Prologue Start to Epilogue End ....
Every word , every sentence
Gives us a chance to mend !!!

The Golden Grey Symphony

The gold and grey Sky ,
the gold and grey Waters -
merge as one—
a seamless embrace of light and vastness.

What is Heaven,
what is Earth ,
is difficult to tell.

My gaze follows the golden hue,
tracing the endless Horizon,
where silence sings in shimmering tones,
and beauty breathes in waves.

The harmony of Water and Sky -
a dance untouched,
a whisper of eternity.

Such peace, such quiet light—
let it remain, undisturbed.

Let the Sky and Water be in sync,
the Earth and Heaven blend in glory,
forever whole, forever free.

Dance With Time

Find the morning light, soft and bright,
A whisper of hope in the fading night.
Find the reason to love,
Find the reason to be,
A melody woven in Eternity .

Seek not just passion—be its embrace,
In little moments, in life's own grace.
Not just in laughter, but even in pain,
In Sunlit fields and misty rain.

The Glory of Life is a silent song,
Sung by the stars as they drift along.
In the Moonlit hush, in the no-moon dark,
In flickering candles, in love's own spark.

Don't just age as the hours chime,
Let your soul *dance—*
Dance with time.

A Walk In Harmony

I walk down the lane,
A song in my stride,
Music in my gait,
With Nature as my guide.

Bunches of blooms,
Vibrant and bright,
Some kiss the earth,
Yet bathe it in light.

Others sway,
In the whispering air,
Oh, what joy!
What beauty laid bare.

Blossoms hang in clusters bright,
some fall, yet bloom anew,
scattered whispers on the ground,
brushing petals kissed with dew.

The breeze hums a tender tune,
leaves twirl in golden light,
oh, what joy, what quiet cheer,
as earth and sky unite!

Laughter Echoes Happiness

Every laughter echoes smile n happiness

Use this to change the world .
Let not the world change your smile!

Life does not come with instructions on how to live
But it comes with flowers , sunsets , nature , laughter n
smiles !

Let each day come with its colours ...
Let each day come with a choice ...
Let each day come with pigments of
laughter, smile n rejoice!!!!

What is your choice ?
For Life is .....the choices we make!!

Beauty in Flutter

I listened to the butterflies
Fluttering their wings
Saying - Have Faith !

For even the smallest wings
can carry the weight of dreams,
whispering hope in golden streams.

Golden dust in the morning air
Whispers have faith !
Weaving its own light !
New Hope Begins. !

Hope

When the time seems to be not in your favour
When people around you are not your type
Maybe difficult to like .

When time seems to come to a standstill
Heart , love n laughter seem amiss.
God is there !
Looking at it all
Surely showering his blessings
Telling you better times are in store. !

A little patience to see the blessings unfold...
Better Times Are Indeed In Store !

Smile

Every Little SMILE can touch somebody's HEART...

Every little smile, a spark so bright,
Can warm a heart, like morning light.
None are born with joy in hand,
Yet we can weave it, strand by strand.

A gentle laugh, a kindness shared,
A simple glance that shows we cared.
Happiness blooms where love resides,
In smiles that shine and hope that guides.

So keep on smiling, let it grow,
A little light is all you show!

When The Nights Are Long

When the nights are long
And days seem bleak
In words -solace I seek !

When darkness falls and days seem bleak,
In poetry, solace I seek !
With

words that dance and dreams that soar,
Let me find the light
I am searching for.

Through verses woven with hope's thread,
paint a world where hearts are fed
With joy and laughter, love and grace,
A sanctuary in words' embrace.

So let my pen become the light,
Illuminate the shadows,
fight the gloom

with lines that brightly shine,
In poetry, true joy I find !
27

Hope and Light

I looked up,
The golden sun beamed bright,
Its tender rays—a warm embrace,
A whisper ,soft, of hope and light.

I looked around,
Flowers swayed in joyful glee,
The wind hummed a melody sweet,
And hope danced wild, so full, so free.

I gazed afar,
Where endless greens in silence lay,
The earth breathed life in hues so deep,
And hope arose in calm array.

I looked above,
The moon stood still, the stars did gleam,
Their silver glow, a sacred touch,
And hope fell softly in my dream.

Unshackled - Journey to Inner Freedom

Journey To Inner Freedom

How I was encumbered by do's and don'ts—
Some taught me,
Some pulled me down.

Now,
As I travel through life, I see
Fewer rules binding me.
Not the chains the world bestows,
But the path my own heart knows.

Let not others draw your lines,
Nor dim the light that in you shines.
Make your rules, dance your way,
Own your Night , shape your Day.

Perfection

Perfection is boring
Perfection is over rated.
It is the flaws which make me
Me for what I am
You for what you are. !!

Perfection is dull,
a tale too neat,
no cracks to tell,
no heart to beat.

It's the flaws that dance,
the scars that shine,
they make you 'You '
they make me 'Me '!!

Thankyou

Thank You to those who doubted, who looked away,
Who thought I'd stumble, lose my way—
Thank you -for the road was long,
Yet here I stand, steady and strong.

To those who whispered, *"Not enough,"*
Who saw my path as steep and rough—
Thank you, for you couldn't see
The quiet strength that grew in me.

To those who thought I'd turn around,
Who never thought I'd leave the ground—
Thank you, for your disbelief
Became my Strength: to my Relief .

To those who said, *"You'll never be,"*
Who never placed their trust in me—
Thank you, for I proved them wrong
And came out really strong.

And most of all, to those unsure,
Who meant no harm, yet closed the door—
Thank you, for I found my way,
And walked right through to Brighter Days !

www.ingramcontent.com/pod-product-compliance
Lightning Source LLC
La Vergne TN
LVHW010928200726
843509LV00013B/2129